What If We Do N**O**THING**?**

EARTH'S WATER CRISIS

Rob Bowden

**Consultant: Mike Edwards, Research Director
at the Oxford Centre for Water Research,
Oxford University**

WORLD ALMANAC® LIBRARY

Please visit our web site at: www.garethstevens.com
For a free color catalog describing World Almanac® Library's list of
high-quality books and multimedia programs, call 1-800-542-2595 (USA)
or 1-800-387-3178 (Canada). Gareth Stevens Publishing's fax: (877) 542-2596

Library of Congress Cataloging-in-Publication Data

Bowden, Rob.
    Earth's water crisis / Rob Bowden.
        p. cm. – (What if we do nothing?)
    Includes bibliographical references and index.
    ISBN-10: 0-8368-7754-3   ISBN-13: 978-0-8368-7754-0 (lib. bdg.)
    ISBN-10: 0-8368-8154-0   ISBN-13: 978-0-8368-8154-7 (softcover)
    1. Water supply.   2. Water conservation.   3. Water quality.   I. Title.
TD348.B66 2007
333.91–dc22   2006030449

First published in 2007 by
World Almanac® Library
An Imprint of Gareth Stevens Publishing
1 Reader's Digest Rd.
Pleasantville, NY 10570-7000 USA

Produced by Arcturus Publishing Limited
Editor: Alex Woolf
Designer: Peta Morey
Picture researcher: Glass Onion Pictures

World Almanac® Library editorial direction: Valerie J. Weber
World Almanac® Library editor: Leifa Butrick
World Almanac® Library art direction: Tammy West
World Almanac® Library graphic design: Charlie Dahl
World Almanac® Library production: Jessica Yanke and Robert Kraus

Picture credits: CORBIS: 32 (Caroline Penn), 34 (Faisal Mahmood/Reuters).NASA: 5 (Reto
Stöckli/Robert Simmon/MODIS/USGS/Defense Meteorological Program).Rex Features: 8 (Wildtrack
Media), 11 (Sipa Press), 14 (Sipa Press), 16 (Sipa Press), 28 (Phil Ball), 36 (N. Bostram/IBL).Still
Pictures: 7 (Nutta Yooyean/UNEP), 13 (Gil Moti), 18 (Mark Edwards), 21 (Joerg Boethling), 23 (Mark
Shenley), 25 (B. Blume/UNEP), 27 (Gil Moti), 30 (Mark Edwards), 38 (Jorgen Schytte), 40 (Jorgen
Schytte), 42 (Ron Giling/Lineair), 44 (Bojan Brecelj).

Printed in the United States of America

    3 4 5 6 7 8 9 10 09 08

Contents

CHAPTER 1

Water Crisis

It is May 2020, and world leaders have gathered in Shanghai, China, for an important international meeting. Their discussion topics include a major war, the annual deaths of millions of innocent people, and illness among hundreds of millions of others. This discussion is not the result of the outbreak of nuclear war or a biological terrorist attack. The leaders are discussing water.

Back in the 1990s, scientists and environmentalists began to warn political leaders about a possible water crisis in the early twenty-first century, but leaders were slow to take action. As a result, access to water has caused several wars, including a major conflict between Ethiopia and Egypt over the use of the Nile River's waters. More than 1 billion people often become sick because they do not have clean water or a sanitary way to get rid of waste. As many as 4 billion people (more than half the people in the world) live in countries where people do not have enough water to live comfortably. Their water supply is very hard to get (scarce) or just barely enough (stressed). As world leaders search for a solution, many people still take water for granted.

Fortunately, this meeting has not been necessary yet, but the warnings should be taken seriously. Many water experts believe that water supplies are at a critical point. If we do nothing, wars about water could be common, and people could be dying all over the world from lack of water.

The Importance of Water

Water is vital for almost all life on Earth. As humans, we can go many days without food, but without water, we would die in just forty-eight hours. In fact, in some very harsh conditions, such as extreme heat, we may only have a few hours' survival time without water. Water is so important because it makes up about 70 percent of the human body, and, without it, our bodies simply fail. Most other living things on our planet are also made up of a high percentage of water and need it as much as we do. Some plants and animals have been able to adapt to extremely dry conditions, such as those found in desert regions, but they all need some water to survive.

A World of Water

Many people probably wonder why we need to worry about water. After all, it appears to be everywhere. It falls as rain; our rivers and lakes are full of it; the seas and oceans have water as far as the eye can see; and all we have to do is to turn on a faucet to get a nonstop supply right in our homes.

When viewed from space, our planet is full of water. In fact, water covers nearly 71 percent of Earth. Nevertheless, people have barely enough to survive in some parts of the world.

LEVELS OF WATER CRISIS

These are the four main levels used to discuss the world water crisis:

Gallons (cubic meters) of water per person per year	Classification
450,000-528,000 gallons (1700-2000 cu m)	Water shortages
264,000-449,000 gallons (1000-1699 cu m)	Water stress
132,000-263,000 gallons (500-999 cu m)	Water scarcity
0-131,000 gallons (0-499 cu m)	Absolute water scarcity

Source: Sustaining Water, Population Action International

Water makes up 70.7 percent of the total surface area of our planet, a total of 140 million square miles (360 million square kilometers). Not only does it cover a huge area, but water can also be very deep. Lake Baikal in Russia, for example, is more than 1 mile (1.6 km) deep, and the Pacific, Atlantic, and Indian Oceans have an average depth between 2.3 and 2.67 miles (3.7 and 4.3 km). The volume of water on our planet is, therefore, very impressive—about 356.46 billion gallons (1.338 billion cu km). Earth contains so much water that if you drank the recommended eight 10-ounce glasses of water a day, Earth's 356 billion gallons would last for more than 547 million years!

The Problem with Water

Unfortunately, not all of the water on Earth is available for human use. To begin with, most of it (97.5 percent) is salt water, found in the world's seas and oceans. Humans are unable to drink salt water without expensive treatment to take out the salt, and very few crops can tolerate salt water. Only 2.5 percent of the water on Earth is freshwater, and most freshwater is tied up in glaciers, snow, and ice

THE WORLD'S WATER

Salt water	% of total water
Oceans/seas	96.54
Saline/brackish groundwater	0.93
Saltwater lakes	0.006
Freshwater	
Glaciers, permanent snow cover	1.74
Fresh groundwater	0.76
Ground ice, permafrost	0.022
Freshwater lakes	0.007
Soil moisture	0.001
Atmospheric water vapor	0.001
Marshes, wetlands	0.001
Rivers	0.0002
Incorporated in living things	0.0001

Source: Sustaining Water, Population Action International

fields, or deep groundwater reserves. The water we use for drinking and bathing, for growing food, and for industry comes from rainwater, rivers, lakes, soil moisture, shallow groundwater reservoirs, or artificial lakes. These sources make up less than 1 percent of the world's freshwater supply, or less than 0.02 percent of the planet's total water.

A Renewable Resource

Fortunately, water is a renewable resource that is constantly recycled and replaced as part of the global water cycle. Water evaporates from the oceans, rises into the clouds, and returns to Earth as rain. Many supplies renew themselves rapidly. Reservoirs, for example, fill up quickly after a heavy rainfall. Other supplies renew themselves much more slowly, however. Some groundwater supplies (water stored within the rocks underground) take thousands of years to be replenished by water gradually filtering down through the soil. When considering water use, how long supplies will last and how easily they renew themselves are important.

Who Has the Water?

Only a little water is available for human use, and that water it is not distributed evenly around the world. Countries such as Brazil and Canada have a lot of water, whereas others, such as Israel and Spain, sometimes struggle to get enough. Huge inequalities also exist within countries. In a large country such as China, for instance, some areas are often flooded while others continually get too little rainfall.

Villagers rest on the dried bed of a local lake in Konkean Province, Thailand. Many water sources around the world are drying up rapidly.

WORLD'S FRESHWATER DISTRIBUTION	
Brazil	17%
Russia	11%
Canada	7%
China	7%
Indonesia	6%
United States	6%
Bangladesh	6%
India	5%
Other	35%

Source: World Commission on Dams, 2000

AVERAGE ANNUAL WATER SUPPLY PER PERSON, BY CONTINENT		
Continents	**Gallons**	**(cu m)**
Africa	1.5 million	(5,720)
Asia	1 million	(3,920)
Australia & Oceania	21.7 million	(82,200)
Europe	1.1 million	(4,230)
North & Central America	4.6 million	(17,400)
South America	10 million	(38,200)

Source: The World's Water, 2000-2001

When we look only at the amount of water available, Asia, South America, and North and Central America are the continents with the most water. Africa, Europe, and Australia and Oceania (lands nearby Australia in the South Pacific) have the least available amounts of water. Asia has almost five times as much water as Europe and six times as much as Australia and Oceania.

When we take population into account, however, and consider the amount of water available per person at a given place, the numbers change very much. In spite of having the highest total available water supply, Asia, for example, has the least water of all the continents per person because of its enormous population. In contrast, the relatively small populations of Australia and Oceania means they have the highest amount of water per person, even though they have the least available water.

A Crisis in the Making

At the start of the twenty-first century, many parts of the world faced serious water shortages. In 2000, forty-nine

An ox is used to draw water from a well in India. Of all the continents, Asia has the least amount of water per person.

countries (including India, Kenya, Nigeria, and Ethiopia) had less than 528,000 gallons (2,000 cu m) of available freshwater per person—the level where shortage is felt. Population growth is another key factor but not the only one. Our diets and lifestyles also have a major impact. To produce 2.2 pounds (1 kilogram) of potatoes, for example, requires up to 400 gallons (1,500 liters) of water, but to produce 2.2 pounds (1 kg) of beef requires up to 18,500 gallons (70,000 liters) of water. The global trend toward more meat-based diets will clearly have a big effect on water use.

Water supply is already a problem in many countries, and water shortages affect about one-third of the world's population. Experts say that because of an increasing population and increasing industrialization over the next two decades, the world's water requirements will increase by 30 percent. Such estimates worry many scientists who believe that if we do nothing, the twenty-first century could see environmental disasters, human tragedies, and even war—all as a result of water.

WHAT WOULD YOU DO?

You Are in Charge
You are a government official who has to address a regional conference on how to avoid a future water crisis in your country and region. Some ideas have been suggested:

■ Invest money to search for new sources of water to increase supplies.
■ Develop pipelines to transfer water from regions where it is plentiful to regions where water is scarce.
■ Launch an education program to change people's lifestyles and reduce water use in the first place.
■ Introduce high water pricing to make people realize the value of water and treat it as a scarce resource.

What would be the most important thing to do? Do you have any additional suggestions for avoiding a future water crisis? See the discussion on page 47 for more suggestions.

CHAPTER 2

The Quest for Water

The year is 2025, and the city of Khartoum in the Sudan is celebrating the completion of the Highlands Pipeline. This ambitious project will bring water from the Ethiopian highlands through a giant pipeline to the people of Ethiopia and Sudan. Engineers have worked for seven years to build the pipeline across mountainous countryside at a cost of billions of dollars. The water will begin flowing later this year, and everyone hopes it will bring an end to the droughts and famine that have plagued this part of Africa since the 1970s. A Sudanese minister said, "We will remember 2025 as a year of great triumph, a year in which we finally conquered nature to bring guaranteed water to our people and end hunger in our country forever."

This pipeline might sound like an impossible dream, but at the beginning of the twenty-first century, the quest for more secure water supplies led several countries to put a lot of money into such projects. Libya, for example, began building its Great Man-Made River in 1984 to pump water from aquifers (underground stores of water) deep under the Sahara Desert.

Pipelines under the Desert

Much of Libya is desert, and the country has very little available freshwater, but in the 1950s, huge aquifers were discovered during a search for oil in the Sahara. These aquifers contain water that may have been there for one hundred thousand years. Now, giant pipelines carry this water under the desert to agricultural areas and to the places where most people live along the Mediterranean coast. The pipelines are 13 feet (4 meters) in diameter and more than 1,000 miles (1,600 km) long. They carry about 1.7 billion gallons (6.5 million cu m) per day. The project is still expanding and will not be complete until 2025. Colonel Qaddafi, the Libyan leader, says that by then, the water will make Libya's deserts as green as its flag.

Digging Deep

Libya's Great Man-Made River is the biggest engineering project in the world and an example of how much effort countries will put into getting water. Libya is not the only country that has used such measures. Billions of dollars are spent every year across the globe to increase water supplies. One of the most common ways to get water is to drill for groundwater stored in aquifers. Many of the world's largest cities, including Mexico City, London, and Jakarta in Indonesia, have aquifers to meet most, or all, of their water needs.

This giant section of pipeline is just part of Libya's Great Man-Made River project.

THE IMPORTANCE OF AQUIFERS

Aquifers
- hold approximately 97 percent of the world's liquid freshwater
- contain water that has been there for an average of fourteen hundred years
- are the main source of drinking water for up to 2 billion people
- provide 99 percent of the rural population in the United States with drinking water
- account for more than 50 percent of India's irrigation water and 40 percent of the water needed for farming
- supply Europe with 75 percent of its total drinking water

Source: Worldwatch Institute, 2001

Rural areas, too far away to be connected to piped water systems, depend on dug wells and small boreholes (sometimes known as tube wells) drilled to reach underground water supplies. During the 1980s, millions of boreholes were drilled across the world as part of the United Nations International Decade for Water. By the mid-1990s, India alone had over 6 million boreholes, compared to just 3,000 in 1950. In neighboring Bangladesh, more than 95 percent of the population relies on boreholes for drinking water.

Aquifers can provide a quick and fairly inexpensive solution to water shortages. Several problems arise, however. Groundwater sometimes pollutes the wells; sometimes people take too much water from the wells; some wells become contaminated with salt water; and some run dry. Nevertheless, until other solutions are found, aquifers remain the best source of water for up to one-third of the world's people.

Harvesting Water

People have harvested water for centuries using several different methods. If you have a garden, you may even do it yourself, using a rain barrel to collect rainwater for watering the plants. In the face of shortages, water harvesting is now becoming a serious option for improving supplies. In Tokyo, Japan, for example, a plaza in front of the city's government offices is built on a slant to gather rainfall that is then used for flushing toilets.

Water harvesting also takes place on a much larger scale, such as in the fishing village of Chungungo in northern Chile. Chungungo relied on trucks to bring in its water until, in 1987, the citizens constructed a fog-harvesting device on the ridge above the village. They strung seventy-five giant mesh screens between posts to catch the sea fogs that rolled in over the village every morning. As the fog hits the mesh, it forms droplets that fall to the bottom of the screen and then go into collectors for storage. The residents of Chungungo now have a daily supply of about 10.5 gallons (40 l) of water each

LESSONS FROM NATURE

The Namib fog beetle (*Onymacris unguicularis*) climbs each morning to the top of a sand dune in the Namib Desert of southern Africa. Once there, it turns toward the wind and tips its body into the breeze. The fog that rolls in from the sea each morning condenses on the beetle's back and rolls down its body to reach its mouth, providing a refreshing drink in an environment that has virtually no freshwater. This brilliant method of collecting water was the inspiration for today's fog-harvesting methods.

from the fog harvesters. They usually even have enough left over to allow them to cultivate crops and trees.

Chungungo's fog-harvesting has been successfully copied elsewhere in Chile, as well as in Peru, Oman in the Middle East, and South Africa. Other countries and areas with regular foggy conditions could also benefit from this cheap, simple, and sustainable way of securing water.

These fog-harvesting screens in Chungungo, Chile, have been used to provide the village with freshwater since 1987.

Desalination

For countries with few sources of freshwater but easy access to seawater or other saline (salt-containing) water, a process called desalination can remove salt to create freshwater. Desalination is widely used in the Middle East and North Africa. A number of island communities get all their freshwater by this method.

Desalination would seem to be an ideal solution to water supply problems because the oceans offer an endless and continually renewed supply of water. The process of desalination is expensive, however. It costs several times as much as other methods. Desalination also uses a lot of energy, so it can harm the environment unless the energy used comes from renewable sources. At the beginning of the twenty-first century, about 120 countries have desalination plants, but the world's population could use up their combined annual output in fourteen hours.

Desalination, therefore, does not offer a global solution. It is important, however, to countries that have very little freshwater and that may not have any other way to get water. In the future, if we fail to conserve the supplies we have, then desalination could become a key technology.

industrial products
10%

livestock and livestock products
23%

crops and cereals
67%

We need water to create most of the products we sell to others. We trade water when we buy and sell these products. This chart shows how the world's water trade is divided by product type.

Source: International Year of Freshwater, 2003

A desalination plant at Dhahran, Saudi Arabia. With almost no freshwater supplies of its own, Saudi Arabia is a world leader in desalination technology.

Trading Water

Some countries buy water to meet their needs. Turkey, for example, sells water to Israel and Cyprus. The water is towed across the Mediterranean in giant plastic bags. Turkey also has plans for pipelines and supertankers to deliver water to other water-scarce neighbors. Tankers already deliver water from other countries to islands in the Bahamas and to Japan, Korea, and Taiwan, and more pipelines and tankers are in the planning stage to further increase the global trade in water.

There is also a trade in *virtual water*—the water used to produce crops, livestock, and industrial goods that are then exported. This virtual water accounts for about 15 percent of the world's current water use. For example, it takes about 275 gallons (1,041 liters) of water to grow 1.1 tons (1 tonne) of wheat. For a country facing water shortages, it is easier to import grain than it is to import the water to grow it.

Water-stressed nations already import one-quarter of the world's grain, and as more nations become water-stressed, they are likely to add to this trade in virtual water. Some of those nations, such as China and India, currently export grain so there is concern that there will not be enough grain to go around if water shortages force them to become importers, too.

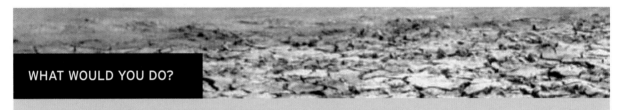

WHAT WOULD YOU DO?

You Are in Charge
You work for a major private water company that wants to increase its supplies because of growing demand. The following three options are available:

1. Build a desalination plant to add freshwater to the existing system.
2. Construct a pipeline to buy and transport water from your neighboring country that has a plentiful supply of water.
3. Drill deep boreholes to explore for fossil groundwater (water stored from prehistoric times when the climate was wetter) contained in aquifers.

What will be the most important thing to do? Do you have other suggestions for avoiding a future water crisis?

CHAPTER 3

Messing with Nature

Nataliya sits on the balcony of her house in Uzbekistan with her granddaughter Mina, who has come to visit. They stare out at the desert in front of them, and Mina asks what the large, unusual shapes are on the horizon. "Why don't you get your grandfather's binoculars and have a look?" replies Nataliya. Mina looks through the heavy binoculars, and, to her amazement, she sees several large fishing boats.

"What are they doing in the middle of the desert?" she asks. Nataliya explains that when she was a little girl in the 1950s, the land in front of them was all water, part of the world's fourth-biggest lake, the Aral Sea. It once had a busy fishing industry, but then the waters flowing into the lake were used for irrigating cotton, and the lake began to shrink. Fishing boats were left stranded, and, by 2005, the shoreline had moved about 150 miles (250 km). "Twenty years later, and the lake has still not returned," says Nataliya with a sad look in her eyes.

Warnings for Tomorrow

The story of the Aral Sea is one of the great warnings to us all about the dangers of messing with nature. It is not the only one. In our continual search for water, we have caused rivers to run dry, flooded entire communities, caused aquifers to sink, poisoned soils, and destroyed habitats and wildlife.

Scientists expect the global demand for water for human use to increase by at least 40 percent by the year 2025. They estimate that providing food for the increasing population will require 17 percent

A fishing boat lies stranded far from the water in the barren landscape that was once the Aral Sea in Uzbekistan.

more water, so it is important that we find ways to work with nature and not against it. If we do nothing, then the disaster of the Aral Sea could be repeated around the world.

Diverting Water

Taking water (extraction) from the rivers that feed the Aral Sea caused it to shrink. Diverting water from rivers does not always cause problems, but when it upsets natural processes, the effects can often be devastating. For more than two hundred days in 1997, the Huang He (Yellow River) in China, for example, failed to reach the sea because too much water was taken from it farther upstream. It also failed to reach the sea at certain times of the year in other years. The Colorado River in the United States and the Nile River in Egypt have also failed to reach the sea recently.

SHRINKING LAKES

Excessive water use has caused about half of the world's lakes to shrink or to disappear completely. Here are some examples.

Lake	Effect of Water Extraction
Lake Chad, West Africa	Area reduced by 95% since 1960 because of many droughts and because so much water was taken from rivers feeding it.
Aral Sea, Kazakhstan/Uzbekistan	Area reduced by 80% since 1960; the sea could disappear completely by 2020.
Dead Sea, Israel/Jordan/Palestine	Taking water for irrigation is causing water levels to fall by about 3 feet (1 m) per year; the sea could disappear by 2050.
Huang He Basin, China	Since the 1980s, about 3,000 of the 5,100 lakes along the course of the Huang He River have disappeared.
Lake Chapala, Mexico	Since the 1970s, the lake has lost more than 80% of its water because of irrigation and urban demand.
Dal Lake, India	Lake has shrunk by half since 1980s and water levels by 8 feet (2.4 m) from 1995 to 2005.
Owens Lake, California, USA	This lake dried up completely in 1920s when water from the Owens River was diverted to Los Angeles. The dust from the dried lake bed contributes to air pollution in L.A.

Source: Eco-Economy Updates, April 2005, Earth Policy Institute

When rivers fail to reach the sea, salt water can flow inland up the river's ususal course, destroying local habitats and wildlife that are unable to cope with the high salt levels. The seacoasts also erode, or wear away, faster because the sand and silt that the river once deposited no longer provide protection from waves. Rivers also deliver a lot of nutrients into the oceans, and fish that rely on these nutrients for food can die or leave the area if the rivers no longer reach the sea. This happened to sardine populations in the eastern Mediterranean following the completion of the Aswan High Dam in Egypt. The dam stopped the flow of nutrients from the Nile River, and the annual sardine catch fell from 18,300 tons (18,000 tonnes) to just 510 tons (500 tonnes).

Many of the world's rivers have been dammed to store their water for human use. This water reservoir is in Yorkshire in England and is very small. Some reservoirs stretch for hundreds of miles (kilometers).

Dams

People have been building dams for centuries as a way of capturing water for human use. In fact, some of the earliest evidence of dam construction in Egypt and Jordan dates back more than five thousand years. Dams let us store water, send it in the direction we want (for irrigation or through pipelines to urban areas), and use it to make electricity (a process known as hydroelectric power, or

HEP). Dams also can protect people from the dangers of flooding, or they can make water travel easier. In the past, dams were fairly small and had only a minor effect on natural environments.

At the beginning of the twentieth century, only a few hundred large dams more than 50 feet tall (15 m) existed. During the twentieth century, however, dams became bigger and more widespread, thanks to advances in engineering. Some of the largest dams are now more than 1.6 miles (1 km) wide and more than 500 feet (150 m) tall. Around the world, the number of large dams increased from about five thousand in 1950 to more than forty-five thousand in 2005. China alone has some twenty-two thousand large dams, compared to only twenty-two in 1949. The construction of large dams peaked in the 1970s and has now slowed considerably, but the World Commission on Dams reports that as many as three hundred large dams are still completed every year.

Large dams control almost half the world's major water systems. They store as much water as people use in a year. This huge disruption to the natural water cycle causes many problems. Up to 40 percent of water stored in dams may be lost because it evaporates.

As the graph shows, China has twice as many dams as the rest of Asia.

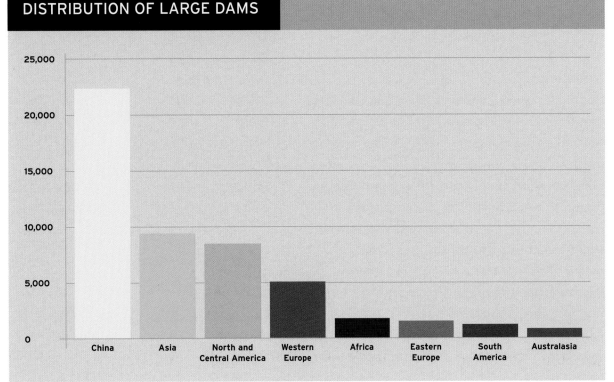

DISTRIBUTION OF LARGE DAMS

Source: World Commission on Dams, 2000.

Dams hold back water, but they also hold back nutrients and sediment. Over time, this buildup of sediment makes each reservoir so much smaller that globally we lose 0.5 to 1 percent of our storage capacity every year. If this trend continues, by 2025 almost one-quarter of the world's freshwater storage capacity could be lost, at a time when population and demand will be even greater.

Large dams disrupt fish populations and have helped to wipe out about 20 percent of the world's nine thousand freshwater fish species. Building the reservoirs for the dams also meant that whole communities had to be moved. As many as 80 million people may have been displaced in recent decades because of dam construction. The exact numbers are hard to calculate because many of the displaced people live in countries with undeveloped economies where accurate records are not always available. In India, for example, estimates of the number of people displaced by large dams range from 16 to 38 million.

Some experts claim that large dams have also caused more earthquakes in some areas. Others say that the combined effect of the water stored by all the dams in the world has even caused a very slight wobble in the revolution of the Earth!

Irrigation

One of the main reasons for building large dams is to provide water for irrigating farmland. Much of the water that comes from aquifers is also used for irrigation, and farming accounts for about 70 percent of human water use. During the twentieth century, five times as much farmland was irrigated as in the past, and today the area under irrigation covers between 620 and 680 million acres (250 and 275 million hectares). This is only about 17 percent of all the farmland in the world, but irrigated land produces about 40 percent of the world's total food production.

Irrigation is not all good news, however. Most irrigation systems waste a lot of water. Water lies on the surface or sinks into the ground instead of being used by the plants. Excessive use of water not only

WORLD IRRIGATED AREA 1961-2002

Year	Million acres	(Million hectares)
1961	343.7	139.1
1965	371.15	150.2
1970	415.4	168.0
1975	466	188.6
1980	519.4	210.2
1985	557.7	225.7
1990	605.4	245.0
1995	648.2	262.3
2000	680	275.2
2002	684	276.8

Source: UN Food and Agricultural Organization, 2005

limits what is left for other uses but can also lead to a damaging environmental problem called salinization. When too much water is applied to crops, the water evaporates and leaves behind high concentrations of mineral salts. Salts can also rise to the surface when water tables, or the upper limits of the ground saturated with water, are shallow or when using too much water causes the water table to rise.

A temple in Manibeli village in India lies submerged beneath the waters that have risen behind the Sardar Sarovar Dam on the Narmada River.

When soils become too salty, they can no longer produce crops, and productive farmland can be ruined. Around the world, about one-quarter of the irrigated land suffers some degree of salinization, leading to lower harvests or even complete crop failure. In some locations, salinization may be reversed by a process of flushing the salts from the soil, but this is expensive and time-consuming. A more effective approach is to reduce the risks in the first place by managing water more carefully and by using more efficient irrigation techniques. Drip irrigation, for example, whereby the water is delivered close to the plant roots through a system of pipes, reduces water loss to less than 10 percent. This figure compares to losses of between 40 and 90 percent through evaporation and drainage using more traditional methods.

PERCENTAGE OF A CONTINENT'S AREA AFFECTED BY SALINIZATION

Africa	19.3
Asia	68.8
South America	2.7
North and Central America	3.0
Europe	5.0
Oceania	1.2

Source: The World's Water, 2000-2001

Water on a Warmer Planet

One of the big unknowns when considering future water use is the impact of climate change and global warming. People have been keeping a record of world temperatures since the end of the nineteenth century. During that time, the three warmest years have occurred since 1998, and nineteen of the twenty warmest years have occurred since 1980. We have evidence that glaciers (one of the world's major stores of freshwater) are melting, and, in some places, lakes are beginning to dry up. In other parts of the world, too much rainfall has been a problem, causing flooding and destroying homes and crops. One of the biggest effects of global warming—the melting of the polar ice caps and the rise of global sea levels—could also have unforeseen impact on the global water cycle.

Climate change is also likely to put further pressure on existing freshwater supplies. A rise in sea levels could cause salt water to enter groundwater reserves and contaminate the freshwater supplies of more than two billion people. Many of the world's largest coastal cities would be affected by such an event.

Upsetting predictions suggest that farmland in areas such as the Nile and Ganges deltas could disappear under rising seas. This loss of land would increase the area's need for water as new farmlands open up that require irrigation.

From 2000 to 2001 and again from 2004 to 2005, Cape Town in South Africa was forced to introduce an emergency water-savings program because the reservoirs feeding the city began to dry up due to lower than normal winter rainfall. If we do nothing, it is likely that many people around the world will face similar restrictions at some point in the future.

Part of the Perito Merino glacier in Patagonia, Argentina, falls into the ocean. The melting of glaciers is a sign of global warming–a major threat to future water supplies.

WHAT WOULD YOU DO?

You Are in Charge
You are part of a team that has been asked by an environmental charity to help design an environmental checklist for new water projects. With your colleagues, you must come up with three key points to go into the checklist and say why you have chosen them.

CHAPTER 4

Dangers to Health

Kai returns from the store empty-handed. He has some bad news: "'Mom, they have run out of water again!" His mother sighs in disbelief. Kai and his family have had to buy bottled water from the supermarket in recent years because their own supply is contaminated, or polluted, with chemicals. They discovered the contamination when Kai's younger sister became ill, and the doctors told them to stop drinking the water from their tap. They do not know what caused the pollution, but they suspect it might come from the industrial plant on the other side of town or from the nearby farms that spray their crops with chemicals. Five years ago, the local water company said that all the pollution problems would be solved by 2020, and the water would be safe to drink again. Their water is still not safe, and some water supplies in the area have become worse!

What Are You Drinking?

Kai's story is a familiar one. Pollution from industries and pesticides and run off from farming have harmed people for decades. In fact, unclean water is one of the biggest causes of death in the world and kills millions of people—especially young children—every year. At the beginning of the twenty-first century, one in five people in the world had no regular, safe water supply, and one in three did not have safe sewage facilities. This latter statistic is of particular concern because human waste water and sewage is one of the worst pollutants in countries with poor or nonexistent sanitation facilities.

The problems relating to unclean water and sanitation are particularly bad in undeveloped countries, but sometimes water in richer countries is also polluted. Industries, commercial farming, landfill sites, and even households produce a daily mixture of pollutants that get into the water system. These pollutants include heavy metals, pesticides, and medicinal drugs. These substances have been linked to cancer, birth defects, and infertility in both humans and animals. Many governments and water companies have introduced strict controls to try to filter out such pollutants, but some of these poisons are very hard to detect and may have long-term effects.

Some harmful substances may also come naturally from geological sources. In Bangladesh, for example, naturally occurring arsenic in water taken from groundwater wells has caused acute health problems.

Chemicals pour from an outlet pipe straight into a nearby water supply in Germany. For hundreds of years, people have used rivers, lakes, and oceans as dumping grounds for waste. This carelessness has created problems of widespread pollution today.

ACCESS TO CLEAN WATER AND SAFE SANITATION

Country/Region	Regular Access to Safe Water Source (%)	Regular Access to Safe Sanitation Facilities (%)
Brazil	87	76
China	75	40
Denmark	100	100
Ethiopia	24	12
India	84	28
Mexico	88	74
Nigeria	62	54
Great Britain	100	100
United States	100	100
Undeveloped Countries (average)	62	44
World (average)	82	61

Source: UN Human Development Report, 2004

Overloading the System

Historically, we have often relied on nature to clean waste water and recycle it through the water cycle into clean, useable supplies. Wetlands, for example, perform an important role in this respect, removing pollutants as the water passes slowly through them, like giant filters. Many wetlands, however, have now been built upon or drained for farmland, and this important function has been lost. In the United States, for example, about half the Florida Everglades has been lost to home building and agriculture.

The earth beneath our feet also serves as a filter. Water slowly passes through layers of soil and rock that remove many harmful compounds before the water reaches groundwater reserves. Today, the natural systems are not able to break down and absorb many of the complex pollutants we produce, and, as we extract more water for human use, more pollutants contaminate our aquifers.

Groundwater Pollution

Because surface waters (rivers and lakes) have become more polluted, we have increasingly used groundwater instead as a source of pure water. Scientists believed that groundwater would be free from harmful substances, but recent studies have shown that groundwater is also polluted. In some instances, naturally occurring chemicals such as fluoride or arsenic have caused health problems. In Bangladesh, for example, people dug thousands of boreholes to reach water without testing the water for the arsenic that occurs naturally in the underlying sediment. In the Hajiganj thana of Chandpur district, in southeast Bangladesh, a survey revealed that 94 percent of the area's twelve thousand wells contained more arsenic than was safe. If

DAMAGE TO THE FLORIDA EVERGLADES ECOSYSTEM

A 50% reduction in the area of the Everglades has caused:

- A 90-95% decrease in the number of wading birds
- 68 threatened or endangered species
- 651.7 billion gallons (2,467 million cu m) of water lost from the system through discharge and unnatural seepage annually
- Increased unnatural discharges of freshwater that have damaged coastal estuaries
- The incidence of diseases affecting coral to increase tenfold since 1980
- 1,563 square miles (4,047 million square meters) of the system to be subject to health warnings about possible mercury contamination
- Phosphorus to contaminate Lake Okeechobee, the Everglades, and surrounding wetlands
- The wild spread of invasive foreign species that have crowded out native species

Source: Living Waters: Conserving the Source of Life (WWF, 2004)

consumed, arsenic causes skin diseases, liver problems, damage to the nervous system, and, eventually, cancer and death.

Fluoride is another naturally occurring chemical that turned up in groundwater in parts of India, China, Sri Lanka, Thailand, and East Africa. Fluoride in small quantities is essential for good bones and teeth, but in excess, it causes dental decay and damages bones and joints leaving people in severe pain or completely crippled. In China, more than 1.6 million people may be suffering the effects of drinking water contaminated with fluoride, and in India, estimates put the number at about 60 million. Children are particularly affected because their bones are still forming.

In addition to naturally occurring chemicals, artificial pollutants are now being found in groundwater across the world. Many of these pollutants are complex chemicals that are extremely dangerous to humans and wildlife. Underground gasoline storage tanks at filling stations, for example, regularly leak petrochemicals into groundwater. These chemicals have been linked—even in quite small amounts—to an increased risk of cancer in humans.

This water supply in Khulna, Bangladesh, is a safe supply, known to be free from arsenic. Many water supplies in Bangladesh have been contaminated with arsenic that occurs naturally in the soils and rocks.

Pesticides, fertilizers, heavy metals, solvents, and radioactive wastes have also been detected in groundwater reserves. Some of these chemicals were banned from use on the land many years ago because they are poisonous and do not break down easily in the soils and aquifers. Because of the slow flow rates and long storage times, however, these poisons are only showing up in groundwater now.

The Worst is Yet to Come

This time lag means that much worse is probably yet to come. Chemicals banned as long ago as the 1970s are showing up in groundwater in the 2000s, and some banned since then may not show up for several decades. This means that by 2025, much of the world's groundwater could be facing serious pollution problems. To make matters worse, the newer generation of chemicals that may now be seeping into groundwater is much stronger than in the past. Agricultural pesticides in use now are up to one hundred times more toxic than those used in farming in 1975.

There are many new chemicals, too, such as those used in the high-tech computer and electronics industries, and some of these chemicals may have unforeseen consequences. We do not know just what happens when various chemicals react and mix, as they might do in the aquifers that hold the water we will drink in the future.

Nitrate Pollution

One of the more obvious forms of water pollution is nitrate

Fertilizers, pesticides, and herbicides that farmers spray onto crops are major sources of the world's water pollution. Rain carries the chemicals through the soils and into local water supplies.

pollution. Sometimes a thick algae growth covers lakes, streams, rivers, and even the sea. Usually the algae is a result of nitrate pollution. Agricultural and domestic fertilizers, human and animal excrement, and leachate (liquid waste) from landfill sites contain nitrates. The nitrates accumulate in water systems in large quantities, feeding algae that form huge blankets known as "algal blooms." These cut off sunlight from aquatic plants and gradually reduce the amount of oxygen in the water, leading to the death of many plants and fish.

High nitrate levels have also been linked to a higher rate of miscarriages in women and to infant methaemoglobinemia, or *blue baby syndrome*. Blue baby syndrome occurs when nitrates reduce the ability of the blood to carry oxygen, eventually causing suffocation and death. There have been more than three thousand known deaths as a result of blue baby syndrome since 1945.

CHEMICALS, CONTAMINANTS AND HUMAN HEALTH

Pollutant	Source	Effects
Arsenic	Naturally occurring in sediments and rocks	Skin diseases, liver problems, nervous system disorders, cancer
Nitrates	Fertilizers, farm runoff, landfill sites, sewage	Blue baby syndrome, miscarriage, possible link to cancers
Fluoride	Naturally occurring in sediments and rocks	Dental problems, deformities, and/or pains in bones and joints
Chlorinated solvents	Electronics, metals, plastics, textiles, and aircraft factories	Links to reproductive disorders and some forms of cancer
Petrochemicals	Underground storage tanks	Several petrochemicals can cause cancers even at low levels
Pesticides	Runoff from farms, golf courses, and lawns; landfill or storage leaks	Possible link to infertility and reproductive disorders; nervous system damage and cancers
Pharmaceutical /veterinary drugs	Pass into water system through human/animal urine and excrement	Possible impacts on fertility and reproductive function (especially from female contraceptive pill); hormonal imbalances

Source: State of the World 2004 (Worldwatch Institute)

Cleaning Our Water

Ensuring access to water is only part of the challenge we face in the future. Making sure that water is also safe for drinking or for watering our crops and animals is just as important. In the United States, we will need an estimated $1 trillion dollars between now and 2030 to clean up contaminated groundwater. In Britain, about $200 million dollars is spent each year removing pesticides from water. A far cheaper option would be to reduce the pollutants entering the water system in the first place.

Reducing pollutants need not be expensive or complicated. Simple pit latrines, for example, are highly effective at reducing the volume of human waste entering water supplies, and boiling water before drinking or using it for cooking can kill almost all harmful bacteria.

Sixty to 90 percent of the fertilizers that are used end up as waste in the environment. Some simple farming methods dramatically reduce the need for these pesticides and fertilizers. Mixing different crops (rather than growing a single crop in a monoculture) gives plants a better chance of resisting pests and diseases that could wipe out a single variety. Crops such as beans and peas (legumes) can also work as fertilizers because they have a natural ability to fix nitrogen in the soil. These methods have

This scientist is taking samples of water near a waste outlet of a coal-fired power station in Britain. Careful monitoring can help reduce pollution.

been used in countries as diverse as China, Kenya, Cuba, the Netherlands, Indonesia, and the United States. In nearly all cases, the need for chemical additions has fallen by about half, while yields have remained the same or even increased.

Industries have also found ways to reduce the amount of pollutants they have been pouring into waterways, and landfill sites are now carefully monitored for toxins, or poisons, that could seep into the groundwater. These toxins can be siphoned off to prevent them from entering nearby water supplies. Many countries have introduced laws to enforce such changes. In other instances, polluters have found that reducing chemical emissions not only benefits the environment but can also save them money.

Working with Nature

By 2025, visitors to the Florida Everglades should again enjoy an area of outstanding scenery and wildlife. This is the ambition of the Comprehensive Everglades Restoration Plan, written in 2000. Besides benefitting the scenery and wildlife, the plan also intends to improve water supplies in southern Florida and filter harmful wastes out of the region's water resources. After fifty years of neglect, the federal and state governments have realized that the best way to improve both the quantity and quality of water available to future generations is to work with nature. This lesson is being repeated across the world as wetland ecosystems are finally acknowledged for their vital function in protecting wildlife and human well-being.

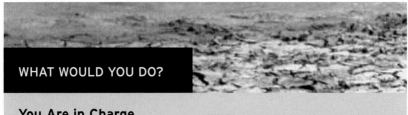

WHAT WOULD YOU DO?

You Are in Charge
As the mayor of a small town, you are worried that the local water supply is highly polluted. You have an appointment with the governor of the state to discuss your concerns on behalf of the community. What issues will you focus on first and why?

CHAPTER 5

Water Wars

It is 2025 and the fragile cease-fire between Indian and Pakistani forces over the waters of the Indus River is in danger of breaking down. Indian engineers were spotted in a gorge of the upper Indus yesterday, which has made the Pakistanis wonder if India is planning to build a dam. The dam would turn the Indus waters in the direction of nearby farmland and further reduce the amount of water reaching already water-stressed Pakistan. Indian officials claim the engineers were just investigating the river, and they say Pakistani authorities have nothing to worry about. Meanwhile, Egypt and Ethiopia continue to discuss their use of the Nile River following their war last year over Ethiopia's plans for another dam and pipeline in the highlands. As a desert state, Egypt is entirely dependent on the water from the river, but 84 percent of the Nile's water originates in Ethiopia.

Looming Conflicts?

These wars about water rights have not yet happened, but tensions that occur over shared water sources are already very real. The United Nations has warned that water must be a top issue in the early twenty-first century, and that if nothing is done to resolve tensions, conflict will probably occur in many places. Sharing water resources does not need to lead to conflict, however, and good examples of sharing, such as the Great Lakes (shared by Canada and the United States) and the Rhine River (shared by six European nations), show us that nations can live in peace and help each other.

The scale of shared water resources is enormous. The 263 international river basins (the area of land that feeds water into a primary river) in the world include almost half of the world's land area. In addition, 70 percent of the world's oceans are internationally shared, which means that most of the world's water is a shared resource. Many groundwater reserves also span international boundaries.

A villager walks toward Bujagali Falls on the Nile River—one of many internationally shared rivers.

Who Has the Right?

The key question for shared resources is who has the right to the water. If a river begins in one country, for example, does that give that nation more right to the river's water than the other nations along its course? When a river forms a border between two countries, who has the rights to its water? These are difficult questions to answer, and they become even more so when the countries involved already face water shortages. Of the ten countries that share the Nile's waters, for example, several (Egypt, Sudan, Kenya, Uganda, and Ethiopia) suffer periodic or long-term water shortages. India and Pakistan, as well as Israel, Jordan, and the West Bank and Gaza Strip, are other areas that face water shortages and share a common body of water.

SELECTED INTERNATIONAL RIVER BASINS

River Basin	Continent	Countries (Those with the biggest part of the basin listed first)
Amazon	South America	Brazil, Peru, Bolivia, Colombia, Ecuador, Venezuela, Guyana, Surinam
Congo	Africa	Democratic Republic of the Congo, Central African Republic, Angola, Congo, Zambia, Tanzania, Cameroon, Burundi, Rwanda, the Republic of Gabon, Malawi
Danube	Europe	Romania, Hungary, Serbia, Montenegro, Austria, Germany, Bulgaria, Slovakia, Bosnia and Herzegovina, Croatia, Ukraine, Czech Republic, Slovenia, Moldova, Switzerland, Italy, Poland, Albania
Ganges/Brahmaputra/Meghna	Asia	India, China, Nepal, Bangladesh, Bhutan, Myanmar
Indus	Asia	Pakistan, India, China, Afghanistan
Jordan	Asia	Jordan, Israel, Syria, West Bank*, Egypt, Golan Heights*, Lebanon (*disputed territory controlled by Israel)
Mekong	Asia	Laos, Thailand, China, Cambodia, Vietnam, Myanmar
Niger	Africa	Nigeria, Mali, Niger, Algeria, Guinea, Cameroon, Burkina Faso, Benin, Ivory Coast, Chad, Sierra Leone
Nile	Africa	Sudan, Ethiopia, Egypt, Uganda, Tanzania, Kenya, Congo DR, Rwanda, Burundi, Eritrea
Rhine	Europe	Germany, Switzerland, France, Netherlands, Belgium, Luxembourg, Austria, Liechtenstein, Italy
Tigris-Euphrates/Shatt al Arab	Asia	Iraq, Turkey, Iran, Syria, Jordan, Saudi Arabia
Zambezi	Africa	Zambia, Angola, Zimbabwe, Mozambique, Malawi, Tanzania, Botswana, Namibia, Democratic Republic of the Congo

Source: The World's Water, 2000-2001

Flashpoints

Five hundred disputes over shared water resources occurred between 1950 and 2001. Most of them involved threats and angry exchanges; only twenty-one actually resulted in military action. Eighteen of these disputes were between Israel and its neighbors. Nevertheless, numerous areas under disputes around the world remind us that water is a key issue. In several instances, competition over water coincides with existing political tensions between nations. One example of this competition is India and Pakistan, which must share the waters of the Indus River. Another is Israel and its neighbors, which share the Jordan River. In both cases, these countries have gone to war several times in the last fifty years. Sometimes peace negotiations replace open conflict, but disagreements over the rights to shared water resources remain one of the main obstacles to a lasting peace in both regions.

In early 2005, Pakistan called in the World Bank to help resolve a dispute with India over India's plans to build the Baglihar hydropower dam on the Chenab River in Indian-controlled Kashmir. The Chenab feeds water into Pakistan's main agricultural region of Punjab, and the Pakistani government is worried that the dam will reduce the flow of water reaching Punjab. Pakistan is also concerned that in case a major conflict arose between the two countries, India could use the dam to hold back or release water, causing either serious drought or flooding in Pakistan. India says the dam will have no impact on the flow of water reaching Pakistan because they will only use it for generating electricity (HEP) and not for storage.

Water officials from India and Pakistan met in 2004 to discuss India's plans to build a new dam on a river shared by both India and Pakistan. The two countries have had several disagreements over the use of their shared water supplies.

Working Together

Conflict over projects such as the Baglihar dam could lead to future water wars. The example of India and Pakistan, however, also points to a way in which such wars can be averted. The World Bank was called in to resolve the 2005 dispute between India and Pakistan because that organization had helped create a treaty over the sharing of the Indus's waters in 1960.

Similar water treaties exist for other shared water resources, and at least two hundred have been signed since the 1950s. Some of these have taken up to thirty years to negotiate, and disagreements still come up because conditions are constantly changing. The Nile Waters Agreement, for example, was signed in 1959, but the population and water needs of the nations involved have changed substantially since then. Egypt secured rights to most of the Nile's water during the initial agreements and even has the power to control the outflow of the Owen Falls Dam, located at the opposite end of the Nile in Uganda. Egypt now faces more challenges from the growing populations of the other countries that share the Nile. To avoid potential conflicts, a Nile Basin Initiative was launched in 1999 in which countries work together to manage the river for the 300 million people who depend upon it.

Similar agreements exist for the Danube River in Europe and the Mekong River in Asia. Such cooperation is essential if conflicts over water are to remain small in the future. The United Nations and other agencies urge countries with shared water to use it as a unifying force and not a divisive one.

WHAT WOULD YOU DO?

You Are in Charge
You are an official in a country that has only a 5 percent share in a major international river. You desperately need to use more of its waters to meet the needs of your people, but you must convince the other three countries to allow you to use more water. What percentage will you ask for?

1. Increase from 5 to 10 percent because the population has doubled since the last agreement was made.
2. Increase to 25 percent because all four countries sharing the river should have equal rights to the water.
3. Increase to 14 percent, based on an equal share for each person living in the countries that share the river.

CHAPTER 6

Making the Most of It

It is 2025, and the town of Tremp in Spain has just received a United Nations' prize for water conservation. In 2000, the town suffered its fifth year of water shortages and decided something must be done. The community developed a plan to make better use of the water they have. Now, people collect rainwater from roofs and store it for irrigating crops in the hot, dry summer. They recycle waste water from bathing and kitchens, passing it through reed beds and then using it to flush new low-flow toilets. Some houses have even installed compost toilets that use no water at all. An education program has also helped everyone reduce personal water consumption by as much as half. Local businesses have developed new practices to reduce water use and prevent pollution of local water supplies. Since 2020, Tremp's water plans have been so successful that the town is even selling surplus water to neighboring towns.

Leaving a faucet running is a simple waste of water. By changing their behavior, water consumers can easily prevent such waste.

Taken for Granted

It would be wonderful if all towns were as successful as Tremp in making the most of water, but, unfortunately, most of us take water for granted and are very wasteful. Do you leave the faucet running while brushing your teeth, for example? If you do, you are wasting more than 5 quarts (5 l) of water every minute—the same as the daily minimum the government recommends that we drink.

People waste water in all kinds of ways—in homes, in industries, on farms, and in gardens. Even the water companies waste water. Waste is not necessary, and in many cases, we only need to make very small changes. Think about the toothbrush example again. If you and your family (assuming there are four of you) brush your teeth twice a day for two minutes but turn off the faucet instead of letting it run, then your households alone would save 21 gallons (80 l) a day, 150 gallons (560 l) a week, and an incredible 7,700 gallons (29,200 l) per year. Now imagine everyone in your class at school (assuming thirty classmates) did the same in their homes. That would save an amazing 231,400 gallons (876,000 l) per year.

LEAKS AND LOSS OF TREATED WATER IN SELECTED COUNTRIES

Country	Percentage of treated water supply lost to leaks
Albania	up to 75
Czech Republic	20-30
Denmark	3
France	up to 50
Jordan	48
Singapore	5
Spain	24-34
Taiwan	25
United States	10-30

Source: State of the World 2004 (Worldwatch Institute)

The Price of Water

One way to reduce the amount of water that we use is to pay more for it in the first place. At the local store, you may pay $1 for 1 quart (1 l) of bottled water, but what if the water coming from your faucet cost that much? Flushing the toilet could cost you more than $7, a typical washing machine cycle would cost $58, and a dishwasher load about $19. As for watering the lawn, that could cost you more than $880 if you used a sprinkler for just one hour! If families had to pay these prices, they would be careful not to waste water.

In reality, of course, we do not pay the same for water coming from the faucet as we do for bottled water in the store. In fact, in Wisconsin, 100 gallons (378 l) of tap water costs $0.15, and in California, 100 gallons costs $0.16. The average American household spends $300 a year for water. The average household in Canada spends $100 because it is even less expensive there.

Perhaps this low price is part of the problem. We pay so little for

Women collect water from a well in Zinder, Niger, in West Africa. Many women in Africa walk long distances several times a day to collect fresh water. When so much work is involved in obtaining water, people use it very carefully.

the water we use that there is no incentive to save water. This is not true everywhere, however. Many of the poorest communities in the world must purchase water at great expense. In Nairobi, Kenya, residents of the poorest slums pay about twenty times more for water from private vendors than wealthy residents pay for piped supplies from the Nairobi Water and Sewage Company. For the very poorest, this cost can represent a substantial proportion of their daily budget. Elsewhere in Africa, Asia, and other regions, people pay for water in the time and energy needed to collect it from remote sources. This job most often falls upon women and children who may travel more than 3 miles (5 km) every day to collect water.

As water becomes scarce, pricing it more realistically may be one of the only ways to make people realize what a precious resource it is. One way to alert people is to install water meters in people's homes so that they pay for what they use. In Britain, water meters are now fitted to about one-fourth of all homes, and evidence shows that people consume less water when paying by meter than they do when paying a flat rate charge. Even so, the actual price paid is still very low. The problem is that water is considered a basic human right by many people, and charging too much for water could prove deeply unpopular.

The chart below shows the cost of agricultural, industrial, and household water in twelve countries. The price is based on cubic meters used, and 1 cubic meter is equal to 264.2 gallons.

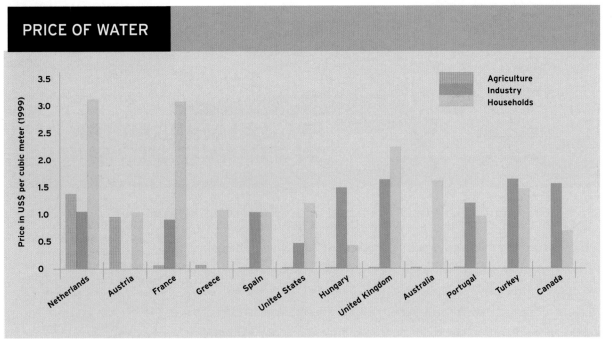

PRICE OF WATER

Price in US$ per cubic meter (1999)

Agriculture
Industry
Households

Netherlands · Austria · France · Greece · Spain · United States · Hungary · United Kingdom · Australia · Portugal · Turkey · Canada

Source: OECD

Greater Efficiency

Encouraging better use of the water we do have could be one way of conserving supplies without having to raise the price of water. Improved water management in farming, for example, has been shown to reduce water use by more than 50 percent. Although some of the technologies involved, such as drip irrigation, can be expensive, others, such as improved timing of water applications, can be very cheap.

Taking a five-minute shower at home instead of having a bath can reduce water use by more than 80 percent. Using water-efficient washing machines and dishwashers reduces consumption by 50 percent or more. Low-flow toilets cut the volume of water needed for flushing almost in half. Special bags that hold about 3 quarts (3 l) of water can be placed in the toilet tank to reduce the water held and

A poster in Bhutan urges people to use water supplies carefully to prevent waste. Education campaigns are an important part of conserving water in areas with limited supplies.

used for each flush. Leaks around the home should also be repaired. A tap dripping once every second for example, could waste up to 1 gallon (4 l) of water a day!

Water companies and governments can also do their part to improve efficiency. In the United States, for example, up to 30 percent of the nation's water supply is lost through leakage. Water companies face enormous costs to reduce leakages where pipes are aging, and such waste seems wrong in a world where many people can barely get enough water to survive.

Consumer Choices

The choices we make as consumers also influences global water supplies. For example, far more water is used to produce meats and processed foods than vegetables. Producing the average North American or Western European diet requires about 1,320 gallons (5,000 l) of water per day. By comparison, producing the more vegetable-based diets of Africa and Asia requires between 475 and 870 gallons (1,800 and 3,300 l) per day.

Many countries now endorse a plan to describe a food's ecological merit on its label to help consumers make good choices. Even the types of plants we choose for our gardens can help: if we choose those able to tolerate drier conditions, we can reduce the need for watering.

WHAT WOULD YOU DO?

You Are in Charge
Public education is considered essential to make people aware of the value of water and help conserve future water supplies. You are responsible for a new water-efficiency program. You must decide which three key messages you want to use in a national advertising campaign. What three messages would you choose and why?

CHAPTER 7

A Human Right for All

It is 2025, and Goreti has finally made it to the international court of human rights. She has come from northern Uganda and is taking the government to court because she says it is failing in its duty to provide her and her family with access to safe water—an internationally recognized human right. The Ugandan government says it cannot meet the new Convention on the Rights to Water that became law in 2015 because it is a poor country without the financial ability to pay for the necessary pipes and water treatment plants. Uganda is appealing for international aid to help it meet the needs of Goreti and thousands of others like her. Many countries are watching the Goreti case because they, too, are finding it hard to provide water to meet the needs of their people, especially in those drier regions where there is a natural shortage of water. The outcome could influence whether the right to water is a reality or an empty statement.

A boy enjoys a freshwater supply in Samreboi, Ghana. Making sure that access to water is a right for everyone is a major challenge for the twenty-first century.

Water and Human Rights

Although water is one of the most fundamental human needs, the nations of the world had not reached any universal or written agreement about the rights to water by the beginning of the twenty-first century. The right to water is mentioned in other agreements, however, such as the Convention on the Rights of the Child (1989) and the International Covenant on Economic, Social and Cultural Rights (1966).

The problem with these treaties, say water campaigners, is that the treaties do not give enough status to water, and access to water is too often an assumed right in the same way as the air that we breathe. They argue that if water were made a very specific human right that could be agreed upon internationally, then it would focus governments and require them to meet the basic needs of millions of the world's people. As it is, about 1.1 billion people lack access to clean water; 2.4 billion have no safe sanitation facilities; and 2 million die each year as a result of water-related diseases—almost four people (most of them children) every minute.

MAKING WATER A RIGHT

A selection of statements from agreements that relate to the human right to water:

"... the human right to water entitles everyone to sufficient, safe, acceptable, physically accessible and affordable water for personal and domestic uses."
General Comment 15 (2002), International Covenant on Economic, Social and Cultural Rights, 1966

"All peoples, whatever their stage of development and their social and economic conditions, have the right to have access to drinking water in quantities and of a quality equal to their basic needs."
United Nations Water Conference, Mar del Plata, 1977

"Everyone has the right to have access to sufficient food and water."
Section 27(1)(b) of the Bill of Rights, Constitution of South Africa, 1994

"In determining 'vital human needs' special attention is to be paid to providing sufficient water to sustain human life, including both drinking water and water required for production of food in order to prevent starvation."
Statement of Understanding accompanying the UN Convention on the Law of the Non-navigational Uses of International Watercourses, United Nations, 1997.

Meeting the Rights

If international law recognized a specific human right to water, many countries would find such a right hard to fulfill. Some parts of the world are already desperately short of water, and the situation is deteriorating. Some of the organizations that oversee water supplies predict that forty-eight countries will suffer severe water shortages in the struggle to meet even basic needs by 2025 and that more than half the world's population will lack access to clean water. In many cases, those countries with the worst shortages will also be some of the poorest. They will, therefore, face a double burden: they will not have enough water to meet the needs of the population, and they will have great difficulty paying for any solutions.

International Cooperation

A higher degree of international cooperation will be extremely important to avoid a future water crisis, and this cooperation could take many forms. Countries with common water resources must reach peaceful agreements on how best to share them. Countries with an abundance of water could also assist those with shortages through water transfers via pipelines or other methods. However, such transfers may bring with them a number of problems. For example, invasive plants or organisms may be transferred from one river basin to the other. Also, the loss of water from one basin may cause springs and wetlands elsewhere to dry up unexpectedly.

A freshly laid lawn is watered in Sixth October City, Egypt. Many people believe water should not be used for such luxuries.

Other forms of cooperation could also have a dramatic impact. Cancelling the debts of some of the world's poorest nations could free up valuable money to be spent on meeting basic water needs. Sharing experience in water-saving technology and practices could also provide great benefits. Israel, for example, has developed world expertise in drip irrigation and is using this method in the Rift Valley of Kenya to help flower and vegetable growers make the most efficient use of a scarce water supply. Countries can also work together to ensure the environmental protection of water resources by agreeing to international standards and pollution controls.

Taking Responsibility

Ultimately, individuals can also play a role in avoiding a future water crisis. The choices we make in our everyday lives can have a remarkable impact, and, as we learn about the value of water, we should make it our responsibility to share that experience with others. Caring for water becomes even more important if you live in or visit a country that is short of water. Many popular vacation destinations are in countries that suffer extreme water shortages and yet are expected to use valuable supplies to fill swimming pools or water golf courses. Water should be respected as an invaluable commodity and not used lightly.

What if we do nothing? When it comes to water, doing nothing is not an option.

WHAT WOULD YOU DO?

You Are in Charge
The United Nations has put forward a new motion that there should be a universal human right of access to safe water for drinking and adequate water supplies to meet other basic needs. You are an official in a country with severe water shortages where many people do not yet have access to safe water. Will you support or object to the motion? What are your reasons?

Glossary

aquifer An area of porous rock, sand, or gravel that stores water underground, sometimes for millions of years; humans have drilled wells into aquifers to use this water

arsenic A naturally occurring chemical that is poisonous to humans

atmospheric water vapor Moisture in the earth's atmosphere that includes clouds, mist, and fog

blue baby syndrome A common name for a medical condition called methaemoglobinemia that deprives the blood of oxygen and has been linked to high levels of nitrates in drinking water. It makes the baby's skin appear blue.

borehole A deep hole dug or drilled to reach water stored beneath the ground

brackish Salty; normally describing a mixture of freshwater and seawater

chlorinated solvent A liquid containing chlorine that is used to dissolve certain substances, such as grease

climate change The process by which long-term climatic patterns are observed to vary from the expected norm; climate change in recent times has been linked to global warming

contamination The act of making something unclean or polluted, such as when chemicals are poured into a water supply

convention An agreement, normally at the international level, between different groups of people or different countries

desalination The process of removing the salt from saline water in order to produce freshwater that is suitable for human consumption

drip irrigation A highly efficient form of irrigation that uses tubing and computers to deliver precise amounts of water directly to the roots of the crop

ecolabeling A system of labeling products according to their environmental impact, such as how efficient the products are at using energy or water

ecosystem The contents of an environment, including all the plants and animals that live there; the environment could be a garden pond, a forest, or Earth

erosion The removal of soil or rock by the forces of wind, waves, ice, and rain

fertilizer A chemical mixture (often nitrogen or phosphorus based) used to add nutrients to the soil in order to promote plant growth

fluoride A chemical compound of fluorine that is used as the active ingredient in many toothpastes

glacier A large mass of compacted ice and snow that contains vast quantities of freshwater

global warming The gradual warming of Earth's atmosphere as a result of carbon dioxide emissions and other greenhouse gases trapping heat

groundwater Water that is present within porous rocks, sand, and gravel underground

heavy metal A family of metals, including lead, mercury, copper, and cadmium, that have a particularly heavy density; they are often toxic

HEP Electricity generated by water as it passes through turbines, which normally require large dams across river valleys that form artificial lakes behind them

irrigation The artificial application of water to crops

leachate A liquid formed when water enters a landfill site and carries diluted chemicals and metals with it as it passes through the garbage

low-flow toilet A toilet that reduces the amount of water needed for a flush

monoculture The cultivation of a single crop species

permafrost An underlying layer of rock and/or soil that remains permanently frozen throughout the year

pesticide A chemical used to combat pests that destroy crops

petrochemicals Any one of a family of chemicals created from crude oil

pharmaceutical Relating to the manufacture or sale of medicinal drugs

pit latrine A simple toilet consisting of a covered hole (pit) in which human waste collects

pollutant Something that contaminates, or pollutes, the air, soil, or water

radioactive waste Waste material from radioactive processes and facilities; it can include radioactive material itself and substances that have been in contact with radioactive material

runoff Water that runs across the surface of the land to enter the natural water system; runoff is associated with overapplication of water in agriculture and often includes diluted fertilizers and pesticides

saline Having a high salt content

salinization A process in which salts become highly concentrated in water or soils, affecting plant growth and even causing land to be abandoned

sanitation The provision of hygienic toilet and washing conditions to prevent the spread of diseases associated with human waste

sediment Particles of material that are normally carried suspended in solution (in water) before settling to the bottom of a river or other body of water.

solvent A liquid used to dissolve certain substances, often made of toxic chemical compounds

sustainability Development that meets the needs of today without compromising the ability of future generations to meet their needs

tube well See borehole

wetland A land habitat in which the presence of water for all or most of the year is a dominant feature

World Bank A global organization that makes loans available to governments for large development projects such as new dams for supplying water

Further Information

Books

Bowden, Rob. *Water Supply*. 21st Century Debates (series). Hodder Wayland, 2002.

Goodman, Polly. *Water Power*. Looking At Energy (series). Hodder Wayland, 2005.

Haswell, Arthur. *Water*. Earth Strikes Back (series). Belitha Press, 2000.

Spilsbury, Louise. *Water*. Planet under Pressure (series). Heinemann, 2006.

Web Sites

Comprehensive Everglades Restoration Plan (CERP): The Journey to Restore America's Everglades
www.evergladesplan.org/index.cfm
The site of the Comprehensive Everglades Restoration Plan for the Florida Everglades, with information about the history of the Everglades, the threats it faces and the plan to restore this important wetland and its environmental functions.

The Right to Water
www.righttowater.org.uk
A site devoted to the campaign for making water a fundamental human right with information on the history of the rights to water, how you could get involved and up-to-date news on progress.

Water Aid
www.wateraid.org
An international aid organization that works with many of the world's poorest communities to secure them basic water supplies and sanitation facilities. The site suggests ways you could help.

Publisher's note to educators and parents: Our editors have carefully reviewed these Web sites to ensure that they are suitable for children. Many Web sites change frequently, however, and we cannot guarantee that a site's future contents will continue to meet our high standards of quality and educational value. Be advised that children should be closely supervised whenever they access the Internet.

What Would You Do?

Page 9:
There is no single answer to preventing a future water crisis. It will require a combination of different measures by governments, businesses, and individuals.

Page 15:
Cost is an important consideration, and so is making sure the water is not depleted. In areas where water resources are shared, the security of a supply is also important. With good international agreements, the transfer of water is a good option.

Page 23:
Your checklist could include the following considerations:
1. To what extent does the project disrupt the natural water cycle? (This could affect downstream users and the environment.)
2. Are the benefits to people greater than the losses that might be suffered by those affected by the project? (Sometimes projects may not benefit many people.)
3. Has the project been designed with the long-term future in mind? Is it sustainable? (Some water projects may have long-term effects that should be carefully measured.)
4. Have alternatives been properly researched and considered? (Sometimes there are better alternatives to the project under consideration.)

Page 31:
You might want to focus on what national regulations there are to control and monitor the quality of water. Are there laws that can be used to help clean up water supplies if they are polluted? If pollution comes from beyond the city boundaries, what will the state government do about the source of the pollution?

Page 35:
The division of internationally shared water resources is very difficult and there are no certain answers. Countries sharing water resources must reach a compromise based on their needs and on the availability of alternatives.

Page 41:
You could choose many different messages. They might include:
1. Recognize the importance of water to life on Earth.
2. Recognize how little of the world's water is available to humans.
3. Consider the real costs of water.
4. Understand the importance of shared responsibility for a common good.
5. Save water today for tomorrow's needs.

Page 45:
Providing access to safe water will be difficult for your country, but water is so important to life that it should become a right for all people. You should support the motion and seek the assistance of the international community to help you meet the targets of the new rights.

Index